MY PIGGY BANK IS HUNGRY!

How to Save Money for Kids

Children's Money & Saving Reference

SAVING IS FUN!

In this book, we're going to talk about how to save money and why you might want to save it. So, let's get right to it!

o you do chores for your parents around the house? If so, they might pay you for each task you do. In some households, parents give a weekly or a monthly allowance to their kids so they have some spending money for things they want to buy.

Sometimes for your birthday or another special event you might get money as a gift. When you have money, there are several things you can do with it.

Spending it on something you want to buy would certainly be fun, but you could also save your money for a big purchase or invest your money too.

WHY IS SAVING YOUR MONEY A GOOD IDEA?

There are so many reasons why learning to save early in life is a great idea. Most people who are millionaires or multi-millionaires today started saving when they were young people. They started with small amounts, but they did so over a long span of time.

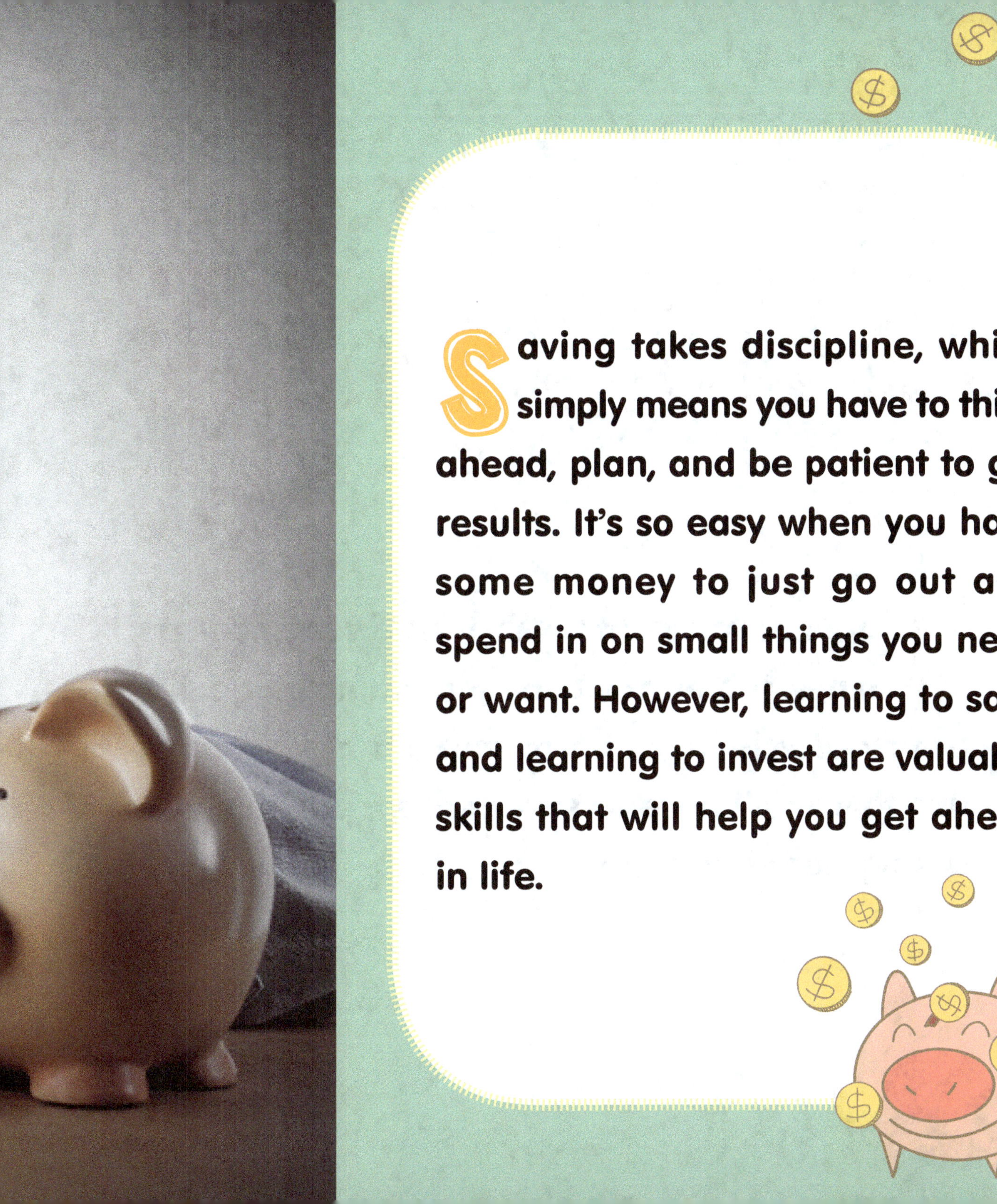

Saving takes discipline, which simply means you have to think ahead, plan, and be patient to get results. It's so easy when you have some money to just go out and spend in on small things you need or want. However, learning to save and learning to invest are valuable skills that will help you get ahead in life.

SAVING MAKES IT POSSIBLE FOR YOU TO MAKE A BIG PURCHASE.

Suppose you want to buy the newest sneakers, a new tablet, or maybe something bigger like a new bicycle. In order to make a big purchase like this you'll have to save money, possibly over a long period of time.

It might be hard to stay disciplined, but, once you save the money, it will feel great to have bought it from money you saved yourself instead of asking your parents for it.

Even if you can't save all your money every week or month, you can set aside a portion of it so that eventually you'll be able to afford a bigger purchase.

Of course, for now, your parents will need to give you their approval for anything you decide you want to buy.

SELF-RELIANT BOY PUTTING
HIS SHOES ON BY HIMSELF

SAVING HELPS YOU GAIN SELF-RELIANCE.

Most kids look forward to the day when they're grown up and live in their own home and have an independent life. One of the skills you need as an adult is self-reliance.

This just means that you can earn your own money and pay your own way without depending on your parents or anyone else. Every time you earn your own money and save it, it's a valuable step toward

the day when you'll be completely independent. This doesn't mean that you'll never need help in the future. It just means that, for the most part, you'll be able to take care of yourself.

When you become an adult and you're responsible for yourself you'll soon discover that emergencies happen all the time. You're saving to buy a new car and then all of a sudden you have a terrible toothache and you have to pay for the dentist instead. When you have enough money saved, you're always prepared for emergencies and don't have to go into debt when something goes wrong.

SAVING HELPS YOU BE MORE SPONTANEOUS.

ometimes being disciplined also means you can be more spontaneous, which just means you can do things on the "spur of the moment." If you have money saved in your piggy bank, the next time your friends want to go to the mall or the movies, you can go with them as long as your parents say yes.

You'll have some money to spend too because you saved it ahead of time and didn't have to go begging your parents for some spending cash.

SAVING MEANS YOU'LL HAVE MORE FINANCIAL FREEDOM YEARS FROM NOW.

Some kids think big really early in life. They want to save money to buy their own real estate or a car or even to start their own businesses and become entrepreneurs.

The sooner you learn to earn, save, and manage your money well, the sooner you'll be able to do all these things.

Some people do so well at financial planning that they can retire when they are really young and don't have to work every day.

SAVING CAN ACTUALLY MAKE YOU HAPPIER.

When you set goals and you achieve them, it can make you feel good about yourself. It isn't always easy to wait for things, but if you're saving for something special and you meet your goal, it's a big achievement and it feels good.

GIRL GIVING SOMETHING TO A LESS FORTUNATE CHILD FROM HER SAVINGS

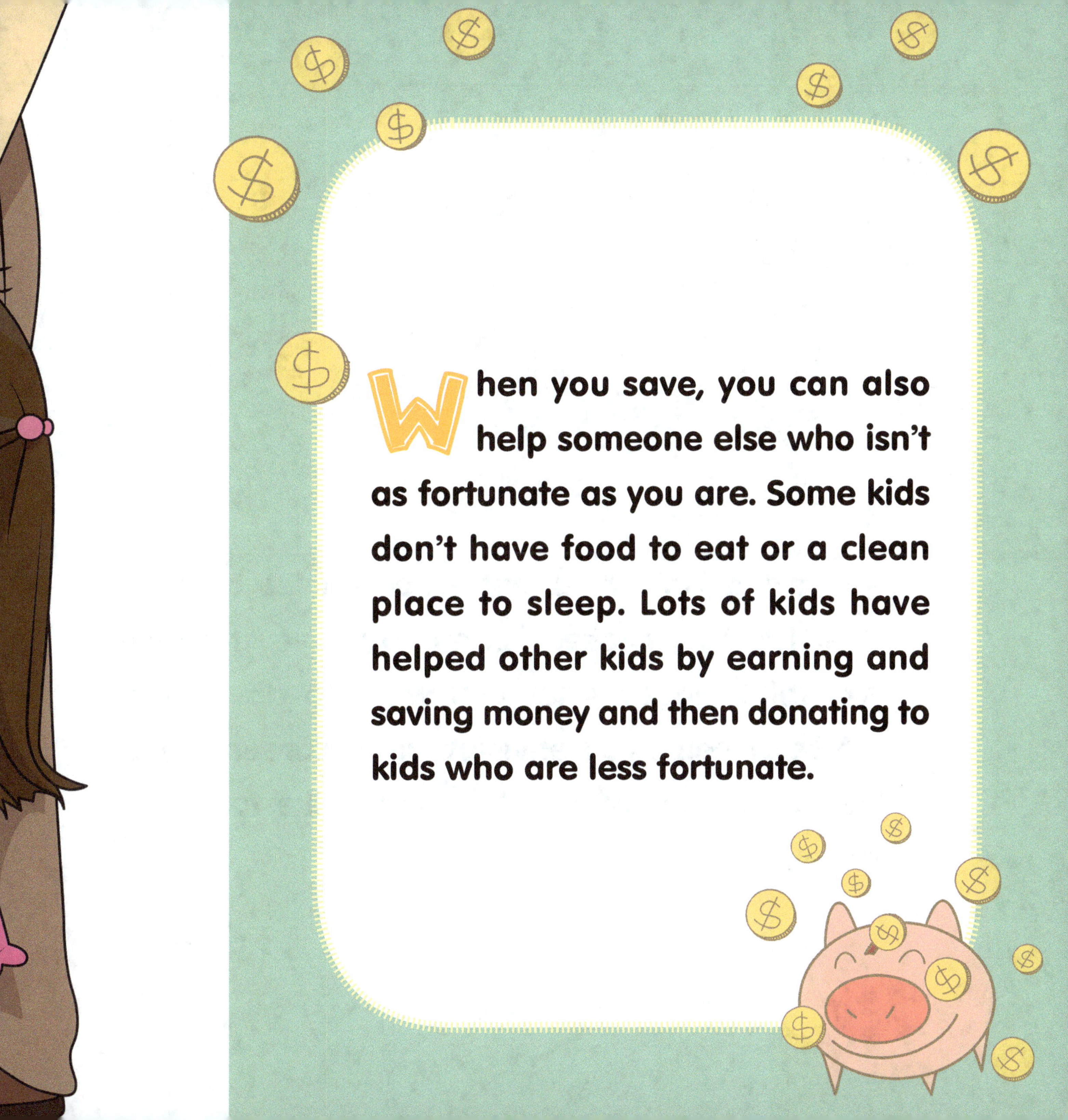

When you save, you can also help someone else who isn't as fortunate as you are. Some kids don't have food to eat or a clean place to sleep. Lots of kids have helped other kids by earning and saving money and then donating to kids who are less fortunate.

SAVING HELPS YOU TAKE ADVANTAGE OF MORE OPPORTUNITIES.

Saving isn't all about emergencies or big-ticket purchases. When you save, it helps you think about what you want to do in the future. It helps you envision what career you'd like to have or where you would like to travel.

Do you want to go on a trip around the world? Maybe you would like to be a pilot and fly your own plane. Perhaps you want to build a big business and sell it for a lot of money. No matter what you want to do, saving and investing will help you get there. Saving money helps you dream big dreams for the future.

WHERE SHOULD YOU SAVE YOUR MONEY?

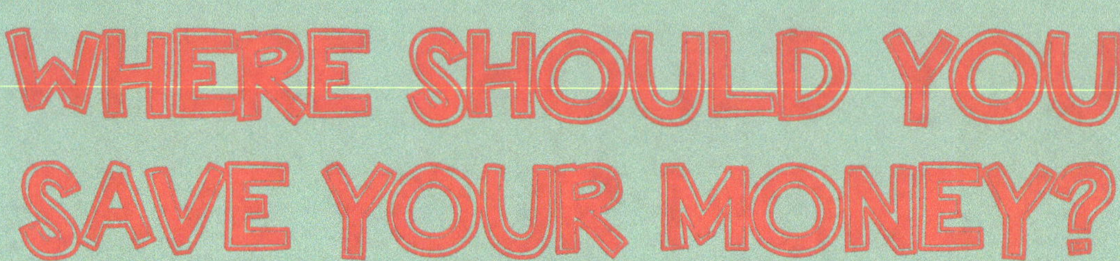

If you have a piggy bank at home, you can put small amounts of money in there to save. That's a good way to start because it's tangible and you can see or hear your money piling up.

BANK ACCOUNT PASSBOOK

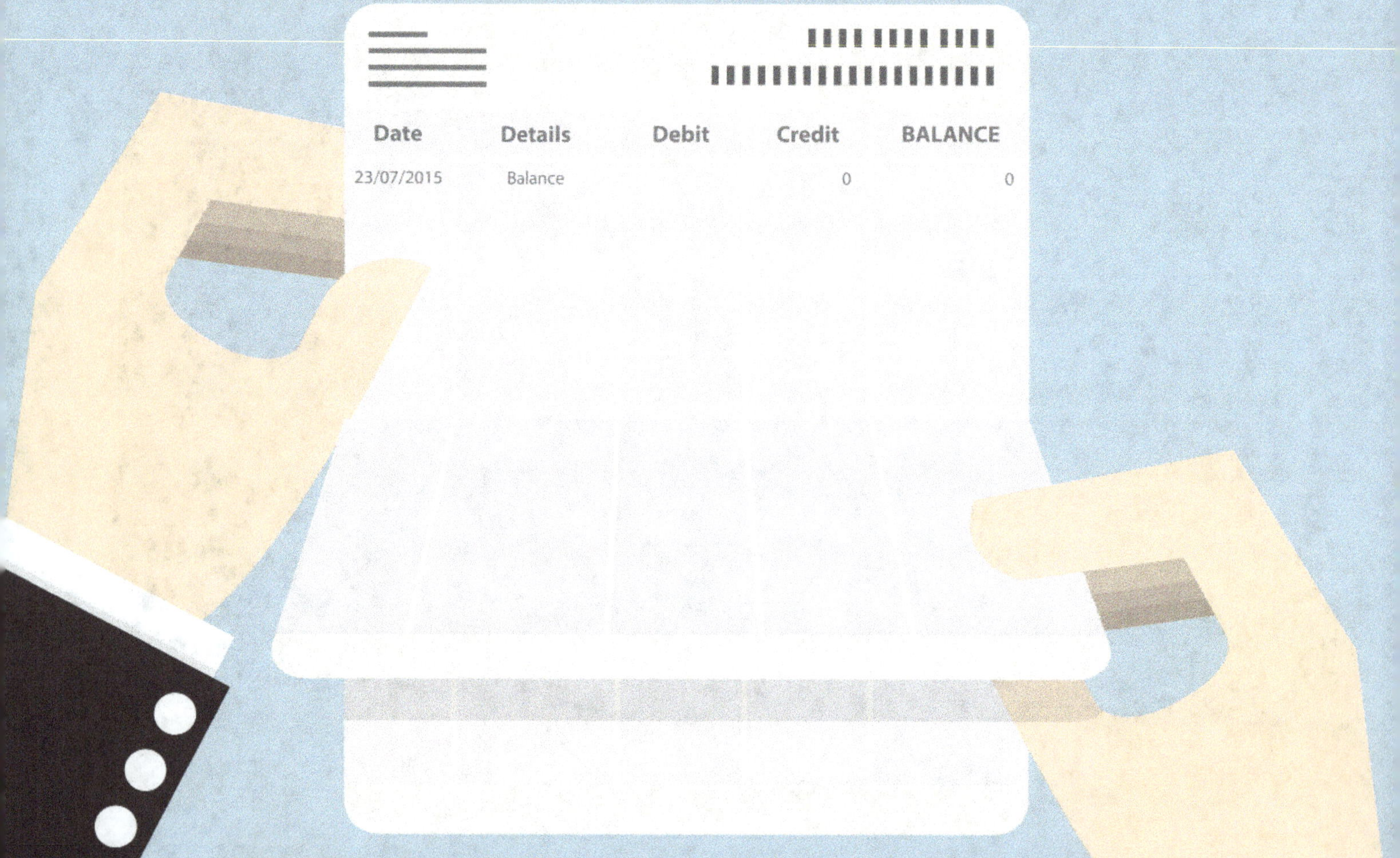

However, if you've saved up more than $100, you might want to consider opening up a savings account in your name.

Lots of banks have accounts that are designed just for kids. Your money is definitely safer in the bank than in a piggy bank that someone can take.

CHILD DEPOSITING HIS SAVINGS IN A BANK

If you save enough, you can earn interest on your money too. Earning interest is a way that you can let your money work for you while it's in the bank. The bank pays you for the money that you deposit with them. The reason they do this is because they get the use of your money while it's in the bank. They'll use your money and the money that other people deposit to make loans for other people while the deposits are in the bank.

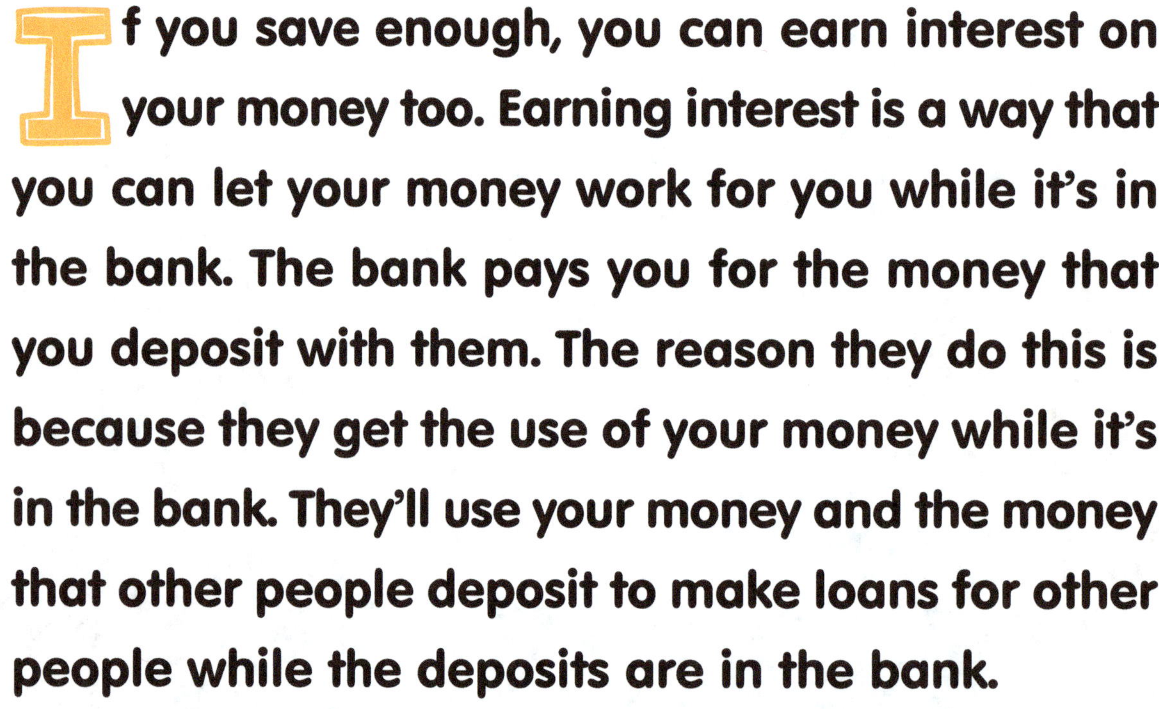

BUSINESS LOAN FROM A BANK EMPLOYEE

Interest
rate

Every month the bank will pay you for the amount of money you have kept in your savings account. The interest rate varies depending on the bank and when you save so you'll need to ask questions about the rates and how they are calculated.

WHAT IS COMPOUND INTEREST?

ompound interest is a very powerful way to have your money working for you. It's calculated on the original amount you put in and also on the interest you've accumulated so it grows faster than simple interest does.

POWER OF COMPOUNDING

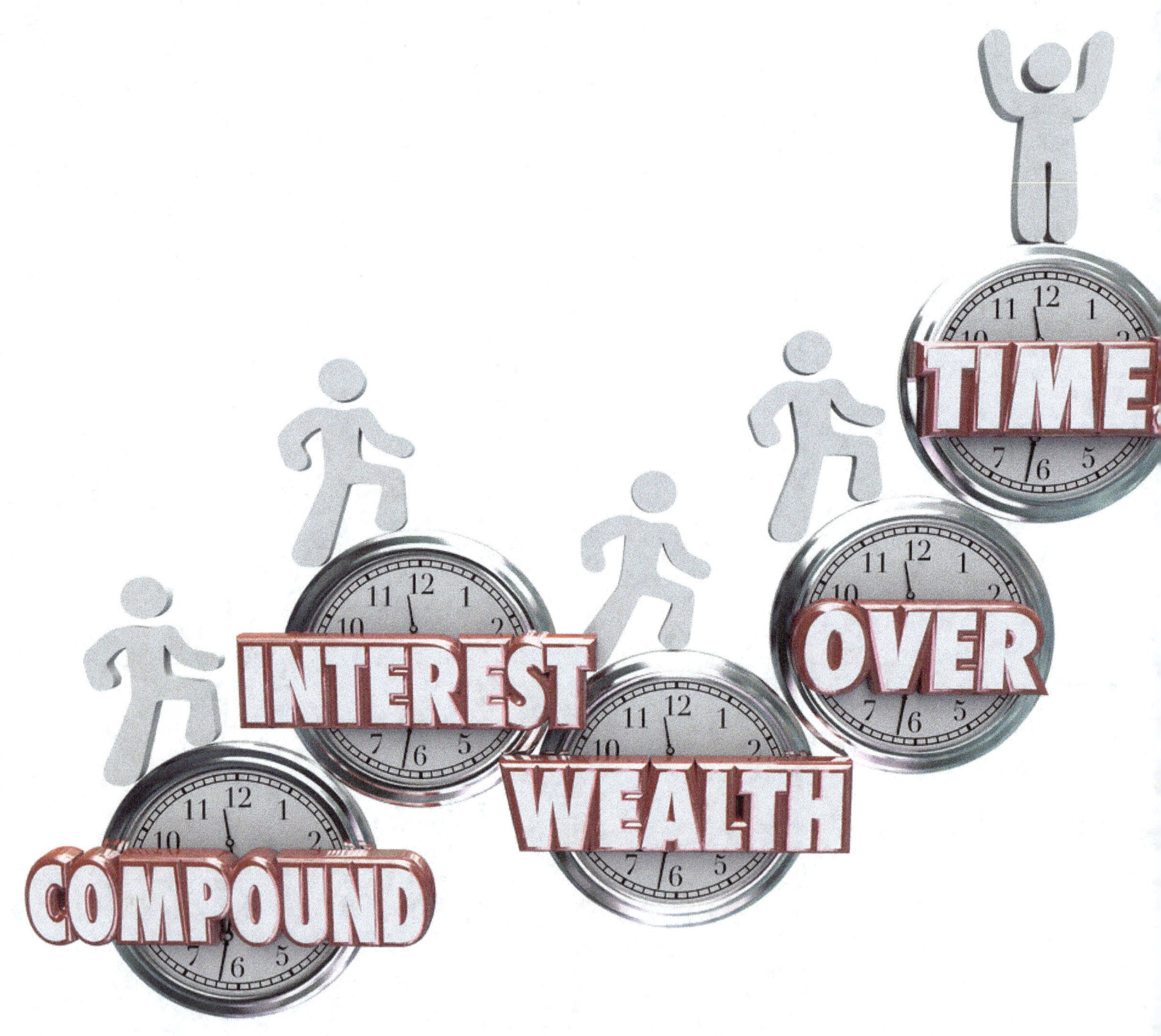

COMPOUND
INTEREST
WEALTH
OVER
TIME

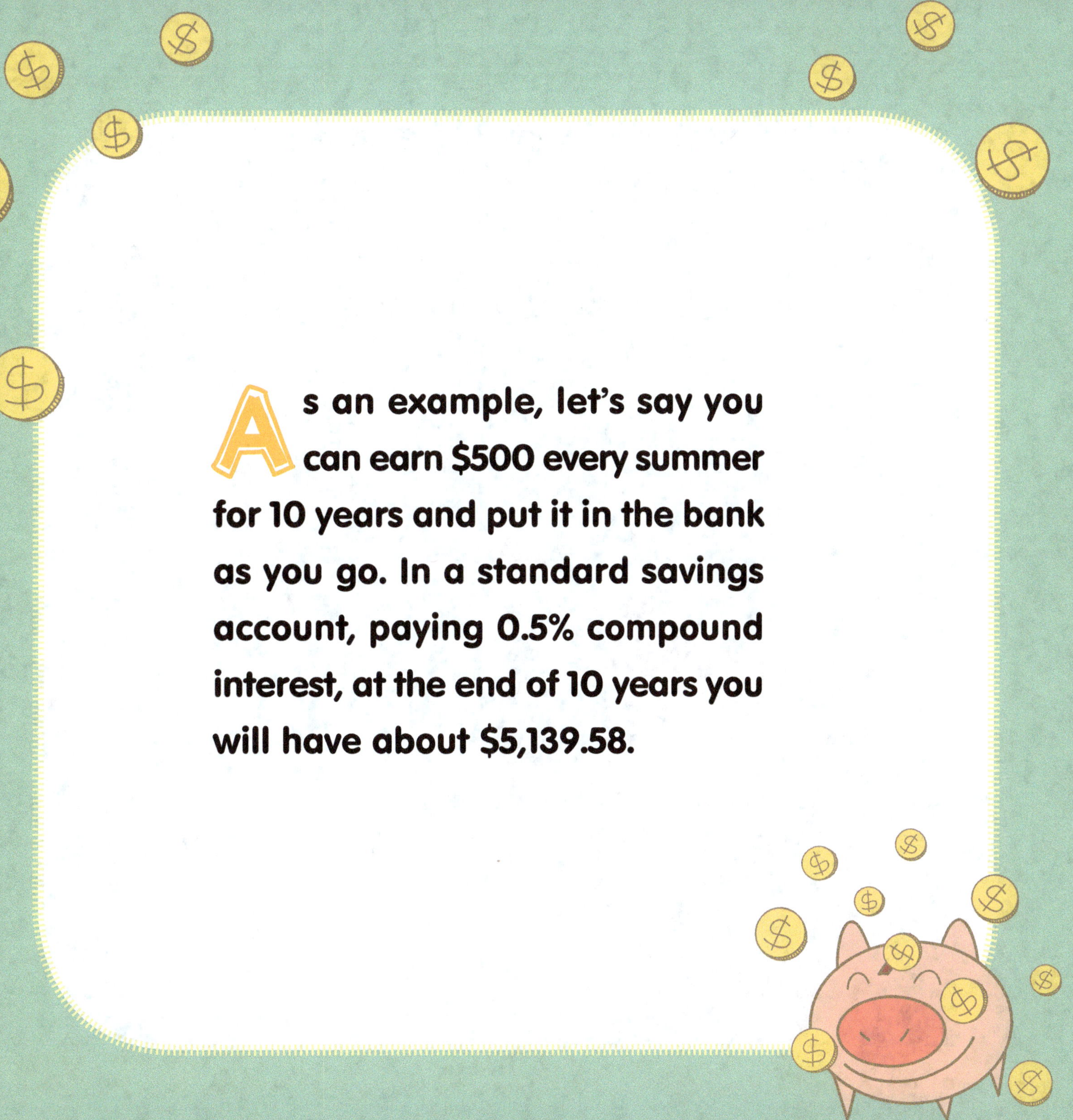

As an example, let's say you can earn $500 every summer for 10 years and put it in the bank as you go. In a standard savings account, paying 0.5% compound interest, at the end of 10 years you will have about $5,139.58.

o, the bank will have given you $139.58 more than if you just saved the money and had it at home. In other words, you "earned" that $139.58 in interest just by keeping your money in the bank.

If you can put the same amount of money into a one-year certificate of deposit that pays 1% compound interest, you'll have about $5,283.42 after 10 years.

The reason that the interest rate is higher on a certificate of deposit is due to the fact that you have to keep the money in there for a specific amount of time. With a savings account you can take the money out at any time, but with a certificate of deposit or CD there are penalties if you take it out early.

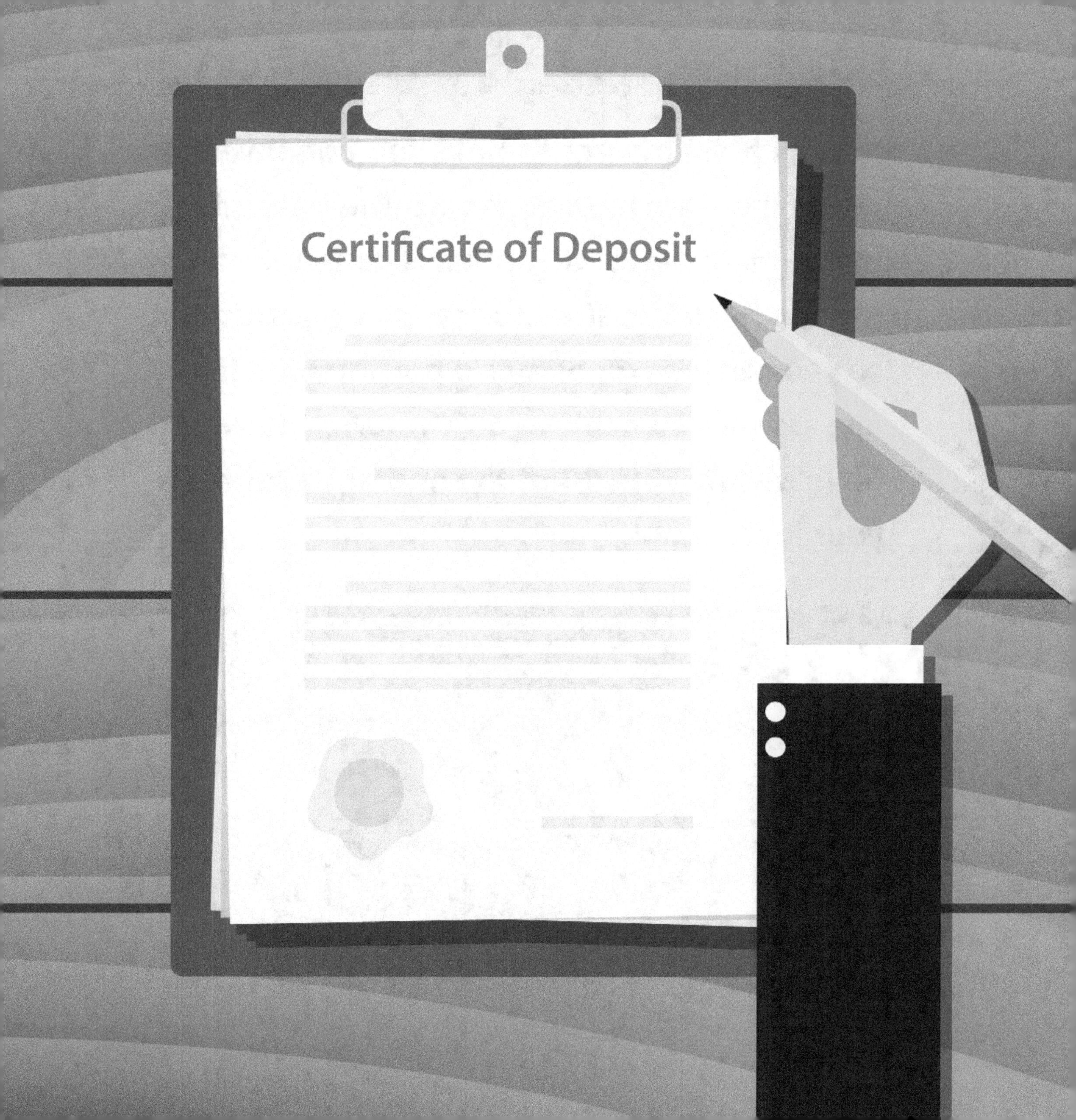

Certificate of Deposit

With your parent's help you can invest in the stock market as well. The percentage of return on the stock market is generally much higher, however, the money isn't guaranteed so you can lose all of it or a portion of it. If you invest well and achieve a 7% return, you would have about $7391.80 at the end of 10 years for your investment!

STOCK MARKET DATA ON LED DISPLAY

SUMMARY

The earlier you start saving money, the better your financial picture will be as you get older. There are lots of reasons to save money. Most millionaires became that way because they started saving early in their lives.

Awesome! Now that you've read about how and why to save money, you may want to read about credit cards and how to manage them in the Baby Professor book Is Plastic Money Real? How Credit Cards Work.